Mental Toughness

How to Build Mental Toughness and Develop an Unbeatable Mind

Chris S Jennings

© **Copyright 2018 by Chris S Jennings - All rights reserved.**

The follow book is reproduced below with the goal of providing information that is as accurate and reliable as possible. Regardless, purchasing this eBook can be seen as consent to the fact that both the publisher and the author of this book are in no way experts on the topics discussed within and that any recommendations or suggestions that are made herein are for entertainment purposes only. Professionals should be consulted as needed prior to undertaking any of the action endorsed herein.

This declaration is deemed fair and valid by both the American Bar Association and the Committee of Publishers Association and is legally binding throughout the United States.

Furthermore, the transmission, duplication or reproduction of any of the following work including specific information will be considered an illegal act irrespective of if it is done electronically or in print. This extends to creating a secondary or tertiary copy of the work or a recorded copy and is only allowed with express written consent from the Publisher. All additional right reserved.

The information in the following pages is broadly considered to be a truthful and accurate account of facts and as such any inattention, use or misuse of the information in question by the reader will render any resulting actions solely under their purview. There are no scenarios in which the publisher or the original author of this work can be in any fashion deemed liable for any hardship or damages that may befall them after undertaking information described herein.

Additionally, the information in the following pages is intended only for informational purposes and should thus be thought of as universal. As befitting its nature, it is presented without assurance regarding its prolonged validity or interim quality. Trademarks that are mentioned are done without written consent and can in no way be considered an endorsement from the trademark holder.

Your Free Gift

As a way of saying thank you for your purchase, I wanted to offer you a free bonus E-book called **5 Incredible Hypnotic Words To Influence Anyone**

Download the free guide here: https://www.subscribepage.com/b1b5i8

If your trying to persuade or influence other people then words are the most important tool you have to master.

As Humans we interact with words, we shape the way we think through words, we express ourselves through words. Words evoke feelings and have the ability to talk to the lister's subconscious.

In this free guide, you'll discover 5 insanely effective words that you can easily use to start hypnotizing anyone in conversation.

Listen to this book for free

Do you want to be able to listen to this book whenever you want? Maybe whilst driving to work or running errands. It can be difficult nowadays to sit down and listen to a book. So I am really excited to let you know that this book is available in audio format. What's great is you can get this book for FREE as part of a 30-day audible trial. Thereafter if you don't want to stay an Audible member you can cancel, but keep the book.

Benefits of signing up to audible:
- After the trial, you get 1 free audiobook and 2 free audio originals each month
- Can roll over any unused credits
- Choose from over 425,000 + titles
- Listen anywhere with the Audible app and across multiple devices
- Keep your audiobooks forever, even if you cancel your membership

Click below to get started
Audible US - https://tinyurl.com/yyxsuabl
Audible UK - https://tinyurl.com/y3wrgnze
Audible FR - https://tinyurl.com/yyn3q6gq
Audible DE - https://tinyurl.com/yynaskzy

Table of Contents

Introduction 1

Chapter 1: Mentally Tough People 3

Chapter 2: Seven Steps for Improving
Your Emotional Intelligence 15

Chapter 3: Learn Psychological Factors That
Help You View Setbacks as Opportunities 29

Chapter 4: Improve Focus and Concentration
for Positive Results with Battle Training
Mental Techniques 65

Conclusion 79

Introduction

Mental toughness is the ability to keep going, even if situations in life are trying to drag you down. Life is not always easy, and unfortunately, sometimes we all must deal with relationship problems, stressful, dead-end jobs, or money problems. If you have ever dealt with these types of issues, you might have felt stuck in your situation, unable to see a way out. You might have felt like you would be in the situation forever. If you have ever felt like this, you know it can feel nearly impossible to make a change in your life when you are dealing with that overwhelming "stuck" feeling. That feeling can be very defeating, and it is these situations that either require us to summon our mental toughness and turn our lives around for the better or remain in the situation and feel increasingly more defeated.

Everyone is going to experience hardships throughout their lives, but it is how we deal with these hardships that can really make or break us. Summoning your mental toughness, developing the characteristics of a mentally tough person, and improving your emotional intelligence are all ways in which you can improve your mental toughness, and in turn, your life.

A mentally tough person uses certain psychological factors and tricks to change their mindset, hence improving their entire life around for the better. By setting boundaries, practicing good communication skills, maintaining a schedule, and employing certain methods used by professional athletic coaches, as well as military leaders, you can change your life for the better and eliminate fear and anxiety in your life once and for all.

You will be able to use setbacks you encounter as opportunities, a springboard so to speak, that creates a jumping off point for you to evaluate your life and embrace the changes and challenges you encounter as a growing point, instead of as a negative setback. And finally, you will be able to reign in your anger, re-focusing it for a better purpose and using the energy you experience from the anger as a method to achieve great things.

Chapter 1: Mentally Tough People

Characteristics of Mentally Tough People

Mental toughness is something that everyone can develop, but it does seem as if it comes more easily to some people. Have you ever noticed that some people can face conflicts head-on, sail through adverse situations, and come out better for it in the end? Anyone who can embrace a challenging situation with arms wide open probably has a great level of mental toughness, and you too can acquire this mentality. Most mentally tough people have similar personality characteristics, and these characteristics can all be developed with a little patience and practice. The good news is, if you're reading this book, you already know that you want to make a change in your life, and recognizing the need to make a change is the first and most important step. You too can develop the following characteristics to improve your mental toughness.

Confidence: Confidence is a huge factor in mental toughness. Confident people can remain resilient to change, because they know they will come out okay in the end, regardless of what happens. Your mental state plays a big role in whether you succeed or fail. Confident people are more assertive and can take charge of their situation to make the needed changes, hence developing an outcome that works out in their favor. For example, someone who lacks self-confidence might falter when making a decision, changing their mind several times or maybe even avoid making a decision in the first place. A confident person will make a decision and stick with it, knowing that they can use obstacles as an opportunity for growth. Confident people charge ahead, making decisions to get things accomplished. They envision an outcome and work toward it. They know that Henry Ford was right when he said, "Whether you think you can, or think you can't, you're right."

Ability to Welcome Change and Remain Flexible

A mentally tough person can welcome change and roll with the punches, no matter if the change is big or small. Change is not always a

Chapter 1: Mentally Tough People

bad thing, and often if there is no change in your life, you are not growing as a person. Life is about learning and trying new things, and remaining in the same situation does not allow for growth or improvement in your life. A mentally tough person will embrace a challenge and adapt to change, often viewing the change, no matter how big or small, as a chance to develop a new skill or experience a new opportunity. The old saying is, "When one door closes, another opens," and sometimes a forced change is all we need to get us out of the stagnant place in which we are stuck. For example, in today's economy, jobs and businesses are constantly changing and restructuring. When companies downsize or restructure, employees are faced with job loss, and this can sometimes be devastating. A mentally strong person will seize the opportunity to improve their life by weighing all of their options. If a mentally strong person who had been considering a career change is suddenly faced with losing their job, he or she will take this time to develop their skill set, return to school, or polish their resume to make a career change. Maybe the mentally strong person had been considering starting their own business but didn't have the time or the knowledge to make it happen. This person will view their sudden abundance of extra time as a chance to grow and develop as a person, starting their business and making things happen, instead of lounging in front of the television, crying relentlessly about their situation.

Refuse to Let Fear Hold Them Back

A mentally tough person does not let fear hold them back. Everyone must go through challenges in life, and it is how we view those challenges that can shape our lives for the better. Change is scary, but so is remaining in the same stagnant situation indefinitely. Moving to a new city, completely changing careers, or leaving a relationship can be scary, but the reality is, you are considering this change for a reason. Maybe you're unhappy with the job opportunities in your small town, maybe there is no room for growth in your current career, or maybe you and your partner have some differences that cannot be resolved with a compromise. Whatever the situation is, a mentally strong person does not let fear of the unknown hold them back. Think about the area in your life in which you want to

Chapter 1: Mentally Tough People

make a change. Now think about how you would feel if you are in this exact same situation in a year, two years, or even five years from now. Will you be even more miserable? Even though change can be terrifying, it is often even more terrifying to remain stuck in the same situation indefinitely, all because you fear the unknown. A mentally tough person would rather be scared for a short amount of time while they are going through a change in life than live in fear of the change, never improving or bettering their situation.

Will Not Let Toxic People Affect Them

A toxic person is someone who ruins the environment or the atmosphere for those around them. The toxic person might be incredibly jealous, judgmental, or just negative overall. A toxic person is like the grown-up version of the playground bully: he or she has low self-esteem and is so unhappy with their own lives, so they are constantly trying to bring others down to their level. The toxic person might discredit all of your ideas or find something that can go wrong in every situation. The toxic person is usually projecting their own insecurities onto you, sometimes unknowingly. The toxic person is not a mentally healthy person and can quickly drag others down. Someone who is mentally strong will avoid this type of person in general, or at the very least, not let the toxic person's opinions bother them. In some situations, it is impossible to avoid toxic people. If there is a toxic person in your workplace, odds are you can't avoid this person at all times. A mentally strong person realizes this and will do their best to see things from the toxic person's point of view if possible. A mentally strong person also realizes that the toxic person is unhappy, so he or she will not let the toxic opinions and attitude affect them and their work. Although the mentally strong person might not agree with the toxic person's opinion, the mentally strong person will listen to the toxic person's opinion and does not engage in an argument. The mentally strong person has the knowledge and the self-esteem to treat everyone with respect, even if they do not agree with what is being said. The mentally strong person knows that the toxic person is just that, toxic, and he or she will not let this person ruin their day or the outcome of a situation.

Chapter 1: Mentally Tough People

Exert Assertiveness

A mentally strong person is assertive. They say what they mean, and they mean what they say. They know how to use concise language so that the meaning of their words is not mistaken and their intentions are not taken the wrong way. Mentally strong people know how to say no. They know that it's ok to take time to themselves, whether that means saying no to an invitation they don't want to accept or simply staying in on a Saturday night to recharge. Mentally strong people also know when to set boundaries. For example, if someone asks them a personal question and they don't want to answer the question, the mentally strong person will have no problem saying that they are uncomfortable answering the question. A mentally strong person can stick up for themselves and does not let other people take advantage of them.

The Difference Between Being Mentally Strong and Acting Tough

A person who is "acting tough" is most likely someone who in reality is not mentally strong. The tough person uses intimidation tactics to fake their own mental strength. They might bully other people by taking control of a situation, or they might simply demand that things go their way, never willing to compromise or listen to anyone else's opinion. If you are working on a project that requires everyone to collaborate and discuss solutions for a mutually agreeable outcome, yet there is one person who insists that everything goes his or her way, that person is probably just acting tough and in all actuality, is insecure. As previously discussed, a mentally strong person can remain flexible in most situations, embraces change and welcomes challenges, and can put themselves in someone else's shoes to better understand another viewpoint. Tough people live to feel powerful, and to a tough person, being in charge, running the show, and bossing people around makes them feel powerful. Although this toughness may make someone seem invincible at first glance, the tough-acting person only sees one way in which to solve a problem: their way. If their way does not work to solve said problem or complete a task, the tough-acting person will be devastated. A tough-acting person does not embrace change or view failure as a chance to develop because they do not have the ability to

Chapter 1: Mentally Tough People

see how their perceived failure can help them grow. The tough-acting person only sees one thing: failure. Their ego is damaged, and they are unable to embrace the challenge to learn the lesson of how things can be improved for next time. A mentally strong person knows there is more than one way to solve a problem. He or she not only welcomes other people's viewpoints but will use a failure as a chance to grow and develop, constantly improving themselves as a person. They will take other opinions into consideration and try to see things from all angles.

How Emotional Intelligence Affects the Ability to be Mentally Strong

Emotional intelligence is the ability to understand and demonstrate emotions in a mature, acceptable manner. Someone who is emotionally intelligent can recognize and classify the feelings that he or she is experiencing at any given time. An emotionally intelligent person can also recognize why they are feeling their emotions and make appropriate changes in their life to feel their intended emotions. For example, if an emotionally intelligent person encounters someone who is rude to them, the emotionally intelligent person can recognize that they are feeling offended because a rude comment was made, and then will remove themselves from the company of the rude person. The emotionally intelligent person also can recognize that it is the rude person who is in the wrong, and not themselves. Furthermore, the emotionally intelligent person will not take the "bait" for an argument, yelling back or letting the rude person antagonize them. They will simply set boundaries and move on, recognizing that the other person was in the wrong.

Although emotional intelligence and mental strength go hand in hand, they are not quite the same thing. Emotional intelligence is a key component of mental strength. As previously discussed, the mentally strong person will embrace challenges, can put themselves in others' shoes, and can distance themselves from toxic people. It takes emotional intelligence to recognize when someone else is in the wrong. A mentally strong person can adapt to change, distance themselves from toxic people, exert confidence and assertiveness, and not let fear hold them back. It takes emotional intelligence

Chapter 1: Mentally Tough People

to recognize all of these situations and to process the feelings and actions that go along with these circumstances in an appropriate manner.

Chapter 2:
Seven Steps for Improving Your Emotional Intelligence

Emotional intelligence is paramount to living a happy, healthy life. It may seem like some people are born with confidence, or that some people are predisposed to a high level of emotional intelligence, and depending on the environment in which someone grew up, their background and life experiences, emotional intelligence may come easier to some people than it does to others. Some people need to work much harder than others to get and maintain a healthy level of emotional intelligence. Luckily, there are ways to improve your emotional intelligence, and all it takes is a little practice and some self-awareness. Emotional intelligence can be improved upon in many ways, but here are seven methods that you should make a habit of practicing.

Mental Toughness

Believe Your Intuition

Intuition is that little gut feeling you have, that nagging in the back of your mind, when you are trying to make a decision or decide whether or not to trust a situation. Our gut feelings or intuition are often based on past experiences in similar situations. Your gut is telling you something for a reason, and more often than not it tends to be correct. While some people dismiss this feeling, intuitive people listen to what their mind is trying to tell them. If you have ever had to make a decision and were leaning heavily towards one outcome, or if you've ever been in a situation where your stomach was upset, and you felt nervous, that was your intuition trying to tell you something. There are countless stories of people who have done something that proved to be beneficial in the end, yet couldn't explain why they acted the way they did at the time. Perhaps someone impulsively decided to take a different route to work, but couldn't decide what made them decide to take an outer road instead of the highway, only to find out later that they made the right decision because there was a major accident on their usual route to work. Not only did the intuitive person avoid sitting in traffic,

Chapter 2: Seven Steps for Improving Your Emotional Intelligence

but he or she may also have prevented themselves from being involved in a serious or fatal accident. Unexplained decisions or events such as these are your intuition at work.

Intuition is a sign of emotional intelligence. You can improve your intuition by taking the time to spend alone, concentrating on your thoughts, journaling, and paying attention to what your mind is trying to tell you. The mind is a powerful thing, if only we let it work to its full capacity. The more you pay attention to your thoughts, the stronger your intuition will become.

Set Boundaries

Any relationship, whether it's a romantic relationship, a relationship between co-workers, a friendship, or a family relationship, should have healthy boundaries. An emotionally intelligent person recognizes their own feelings and can determine if someone else's inappropriate words or actions are causing them to feel uncomfortable. An emotionally intelligent person knows what they are willing to put up with, and what behaviors are intolerable. An emotionally intelligent person is direct and will tell someone if their language or behavior is making them uncomfortable because they can recognize their own feelings and are in tune with why they feel the way they do. The emotionally intelligent person is also able to set boundaries and be assertive because they do not allow themselves to feel guilty for feeling a certain way.

An emotionally intelligent person knows what their values are and will not compromise these values. If someone does something to go against what the emotionally intelligent person believes, there will be consequences in place for the behavior. For example, if a friend continues to cancel plans or does not show up when the plans are made, the emotionally intelligent person would recognize that the friend has crossed a boundary, and he or she must decide if the consequence they wish to bestow upon the offending friend is to end the friendship. If someone continues to treat someone else badly, but the recipient of the bad behavior continues to allow it to happen, the offender is receiving no consequences, and will, therefore, continue to upset the other person with their undesirable behavior. The offender is taking advantage of the other person, who is unwilling or has not chosen

Chapter 2: Seven Steps for Improving Your Emotional Intelligence

to set boundaries. An emotionally intelligent person will let the other person know that his or her behavior is not acceptable. Quite possibly, the offender may not have even known their actions were upsetting to the other person. If the upsetting actions continue, then the offender clearly does not respect the other person's boundaries, and consequences should be enforced, whether that means ending the friendship or keeping the other person at a distance. The emotionally intelligent person has no problem setting boundaries and enforcing these boundaries because they have the self-confidence to know that they are worth receiving fair treatment.

Practice Good Communication

An emotionally intelligent person has excellent communication skills because they know what they want, have set their boundaries, and do not waste time mincing words or saying things that can be construed in a way other than they intended. They also practice good communication skills by listening when speaking to someone. When conversing with someone, the emotionally intelligent person listens to what the other person is saying. They make eye contact and don't become distracted by their phone or other people around them. They listen to hear what is being said, they don't just listen to see how they can respond with their own story. People like to feel appreciated, and anyone who is taking the time to talk to you does not want to be outdone by your story or made to feel like you couldn't wait for their story to end so you could share your own story. The emotionally intelligent person also thinks before he or she speaks. If you have only listened to someone else talk so that you could have your own turn, you have not allowed yourself the time to process what they are saying and respond appropriately. The emotionally intelligent person does not just blurt out the first thing that comes to mind; they reflect on what the speaker said and respond appropriately.

Another important aspect of good communication is body language. Emotionally intelligent people are in tune not only with themselves but with those around them. Making eye contact, smiling, and keeping your body turned towards the speaker are all signs of good communication skills. Folding your arms,

Chapter 2: Seven Steps for Improving Your Emotional Intelligence

shuffling impatiently back and forth, turning your body away from the speaker, and constantly checking your phone are sure signs that you are not paying attention to what the speaker is saying. Not only is this behavior rude, but it does not lend itself to good communication because you are not devoting your full attention to the speaker, which may cause you to miss some key points.

Just as in-person communication skills are vital to a good conversation, an emotionally intelligent person knows that written communication is just as important. Double check text messages and emails to make sure they say exactly what you intend to say. Remember, mentally tough and emotionally intelligent people will be direct with their words so that the intended meaning of their message cannot be misconstrued. Check for typos or words that have been corrected to mean something else. Read the text message or email out loud to yourself if you are unsure of how it sounds. Taking a few extra seconds to double check your work is worth the embarrassment of inadvertently sending the wrong message.

Mental Toughness

Overcome Obstacles in Life

An emotionally intelligent person can overcome obstacles in their life. They view obstacles as a challenge and often have a game plan and a backup plan in case their original plan does not work. The first step to overcoming an obstacle is to break the process down into smaller, more manageable chunks. It is impossible to write an entire novel in a day, so maybe the emotionally intelligent person will make it their goal to write one chapter a week. Likewise, an emotionally intelligent person who has just lost their job might make it their goal to apply to three jobs per day, taking the time to perfect their cover letter and tailor their resume to each of these jobs. An emotionally intelligent person will then chart their progress and reflect back on their journey. Perhaps he or she will note on a calendar what jobs they applied for on what day, or maybe they will reflect on how they can manage their time more wisely to write two chapters of their novel in a week instead of only one chapter.

In addition to setting small goals, an emotionally intelligent person is not afraid to ask for

Chapter 2: Seven Steps for Improving Your Emotional Intelligence

guidance and input, or a listening ear at the very least. An emotionally intelligent person embraces challenges and obstacles but also welcomes opinions from other sources. He or she knows it sometimes pays to get other perspectives on a situation, and someone else could bring a new outlook that he or she hadn't thought of. A true emotionally intelligent person welcomes other perspectives, while someone who is only acting tough wants to do things their own way all the time.

One quick way to overcome an obstacle or get a new perspective is to simply take a break. Go outside, get some fresh air, take the dog for a walk. Giving your mind a break and a chance to think about something else will give you a fresh look when you go back to said obstacle. Upon your return, you can evaluate the obstacle. Is this as difficult as it once seemed? A change of scenery could very well change your entire approach.

Maintain a Schedule

An emotionally intelligent person knows there is a benefit to maintain a daily routine. While in

Mental Toughness

our younger days we might have balked at the idea of getting up early and living by a set schedule, an emotionally intelligent person knows a schedule is vital to reducing stress. Imagine if you woke up late every day with no plan for the day. It might sound fun at first, but the truth is, most people would become depressed sitting around all day with nothing to do, or on the opposite end of the spectrum, they would become stressed out by the number of tasks they need to complete without any rhyme or reason of when these tasks needed to be completed.

If you make a list of all the things you need to accomplish for the day, then cross them off individually when you complete each task, you will be amazed at the sense of accomplishment you feel. Seeing your progress as you make your way down the list not only makes you feel productive, it actually *is* productive. Moving from one task to the next gives you an end goal in sight, and you can see the award of free time, the proverbial light shining at the end of the tunnel.

Chapter 2: Seven Steps for Improving Your Emotional Intelligence

Not only does this routine give you a feeling of accomplishment, but it helps you eliminate wasted time, much of which is most likely spent making nonessential decisions. For example, if you get into the habit of going to the gym first thing in the morning, you won't have to spend the rest of your day trying to decide when and if you should go; you will already be done for the day.

A mentally strong person thrives on the daily routine because it provides a sense of accomplishment, which also boosts confidence and self-esteem. They can see the progress they have made each day, which in turn motivates the mentally strong person to persevere.

Eliminate Fear of Rejection

Rejection, or even the fear of rejection, can be very painful, but emotionally intelligent people know that sometimes rejection is just a part of life, and they view rejections as one more opportunity for self-improvement and a chance to grow. By practicing a few techniques and improving self-esteem, you can eliminate the fear of rejection. The first step to eliminating this fear is to stop assuming you will be rejected in the first place. When people assume they will be rejected, they subconsciously display behaviors that ultimately get them rejected. The fear of rejection ultimately becomes a reality.

Another way to eliminate the fear of rejection is to picture yourself succeeding. The mind is a powerful thing, and if you think positively, not allowing yourself to picture or see yourself in a rejected state, you can overcome this fear.

A final solution to overcoming the fear of rejection is to give yourself options so that if one thing doesn't work out, you will have other possibilities. Rejection from one job interview does not feel as defeating if you have already lined up other interviews, or at the very least, if you have applied at other places of employment. If you are applying for a job, odds are in today's economy, the company is receiving hundreds, possibly thousands, of applications to fill only one position. It goes without saying that the company will not be able to hire every single person. By applying for several jobs at once, or even branching out to consider a different, yet similar line of work, you are opening up more

Chapter 2: Seven Steps for Improving Your Emotional Intelligence

possibilities for yourself and reducing your fear of rejection.

An emotionally healthy person can keep their mind open to new possibilities and different opportunities, even if the new situation is out of their comfort zone. An emotionally healthy person steps out of their comfort zone, accepts new challenges, and gives themselves plenty of options, so they do not have to feel rejected by just one person or opportunity.

Reduce Anxiety

An emotionally intelligent person understands that feeling anxious is not beneficial. It is normal to be nervous before a test, a job interview, or a huge presentation, but when the panicky feelings, upset stomach, rapid heartbeat, and sweaty palms become an everyday occurrence, anxiety is taking its toll on your body and preventing you from achieving your goals. If you let it go on too long, anxiety can snowball and negatively affect your life.

Part of being an emotionally intelligent person is recognizing your feelings and identifying what is causing them. Realizing that you are feeling anxious is the first step. Once you can accept the fact that you are feeling anxious and that it's okay to feel this way, you can identify the source of the anxiety. Begin by asking yourself whether or not your fears are real, if the situation or scenario you are imagining is likely to happen, and, worse-case scenario, if it does happen, will it really matter tomorrow, next week, next month, etc.

One way to eliminate anxiety is to focus your attention somewhere else. Take a break from what is bothering you and cross a few tasks off of that to-do list you made earlier. By accomplishing a goal you already set for yourself, you will experience a sense of accomplishment and improved self-esteem, which are key factors in emotional intelligence.

Chapter 3:
Learn Psychological Factors That Help You View Setbacks as Opportunities

Enhance Performance by Transferring Negative Energy Generated by Nervousness into Shatterproof Confidence

Nervousness can come in a variety of ways. It is normal to feel nervous before a job interview or a presentation at work. When the event that is causing you to feel nervous is over, you no longer feel nervous because there is nothing to be nervous about the task is complete and you cannot change the outcome. The job interview is over, and you will eventually receive a phone call or email to let you know whether or not you got the job. The presentation at work is over, and either everyone loved it, and they will be buying your product, or the entire audience played on their phones the entire time and didn't even pay attention to your presentation. At any rate, the nerve-wracking situation is over, and you don't have to feel nervous anymore. Everyone has experienced nervous energy in some way, shape, or form. When you have nervous energy, you feel as if you could complete everything on your To Do list at once, you have the energy to burn, or you talk fast and can't sit still. You might be jittery, tapping a pen on your desk or crossing, uncrossing, then re-crossing your legs and shaking your foot. It is completely normal to feel nervous before a big event that is out of your everyday routine. Veteran teachers get nervous before the first day of school, and even brain surgeons get nervous before they perform a surgery. Having that nervous feeling is normal and proves that you care about the event that is happening. If you never felt nervous before you accomplished anything out of the ordinary, it would appear as if you didn't care about the situation at hand.

It is how we deal with the nervous energy that can often change the outcome of the event. For example, if you show up to a job interview and your hands are shaking, your voice is cracking, and you fidget in your chair the entire time, this

Chapter 3: Learn Psychological Factors That Help You View Setbacks as Opportunities

will not make a good first impression on the interviewer(s). Even though they know you are nervous, they will more than likely go with another candidate who did not appear as nervous as you did, even though he or she could have been just as nervous, or maybe even more nervous than you were. It's a cruel world we live in, but if you use the tips found in this book, you can change your nervous energy into shatterproof confidence and win people over every time.

Analyze Your Fears: The first thing you should do when you begin to feel this nervous energy is to analyze your fears. What is making you feel this way? Are you truly this nervous about the job interview itself, or are there more feelings attached to your nerves? Are you afraid that you will feel like a failure if you don't get the job? Are you afraid that your family, friends, or spouse will think you are a failure if you don't get the job? Are your fears rational? Sometimes it can be so easy to overthink or overanalyze our thoughts, and before we know it, we have created an entire scenario in our heads that would almost never happen in real life. Take a look at what is making you nervous and first determine if what you are fearing is something that could be a potential outcome of the situation. If your fear is rational, keep reading to determine how to change these nerves to positive energy.

Remember the Positive Side

There is a positive side to feeling these nerves- you are alive and feeling! Although it can be tricky, you must train your brain to see the good in every situation. Embrace the challenge that life is giving you and learn to improve from it. For example, a job interview is a chance for both parties to learn about each other. This is your chance to see if you would actually like to work for this company. Do you fit in with their employees? Does the company operate with the same set of standards and values that you hold to be true? Odds are, the hiring committee has received a plethora of applications, and many of these applications did not even get a second glance or a call for an interview. You have made it to the job interview, which is more than many of the applicants can say! An emotionally intelligent person will use this nervous opportunity as a way to learn and grow. They will view the nerve-wracking event as a challenge.

Chapter 3: Learn Psychological Factors That Help You View Setbacks as Opportunities

The next time you have to go through the same or similar situation, you will be wiser and more experienced, using the previous challenges upon which to grow and build.

What is the Worst That Can Happen?

One way to calm your nerves is to further analyze the situation by asking yourself what the worst possible outcome could be. If the situation you are so nervous about does not end up with an outcome that you find favorable, what is the worst that can happen as a result? What if you don't get the interview or the clients do not buy your product, or you mess up your speech? Although these would all be disappointing, you can still go on more interviews, maybe for an even better job opportunity. You can pitch your product to more clients, maybe even to clients who would buy a larger quantity of your product or who would refer you to other businesses. You can use the speech you gave as an opportunity to practice, and next time maybe you will rehearse more before you go in front of a huge audience. At any rate, one major key to transferring this nervous energy into shatterproof confidence is to ask yourself, "What is the worst that can happen?" At the very least, you are getting more experience, opening yourself up to new challenges, and improving your emotional intelligence by using this nerve-wracking experience as an opportunity for growth. As an emotionally intelligent human being, you are recognizing your feelings and analyzing what is causing them, which will only improve your emotional intelligence, self-awareness, and self-confidence

Tell Yourself You Are Excited

One surefire way to use your anxious state to fuel a successful outcome is to tell yourself that you are actually excited instead of nervous. You can "trick" your brain into thinking that the nervous feelings and symptoms you feel are due to excitement instead of nerves, as the adrenaline-rush feeling of excitement is very similar to a nervous feeling. In both situations your heart is beating fast, your hands are sweaty, and you feel a jittery energy. Think, for instance, how you feel on a rollercoaster ride. The adrenaline rush and the thrill as the cart jerks around the corner and drops you straight down the track can be heart-thumping. Your body experiences the same

Chapter 3: Learn Psychological Factors That Help You View Setbacks as Opportunities

symptoms when you are nervous. By telling yourself that you are excited about this new opportunity or situation, your brain will have a different response, using the nervous feelings for good instead of trying to dispel the symptoms, which can sometimes actually make them worse.

Learn About the Situation

Nerves and the nervous feeling you get from certain situations are often based on the unknown. In reality, there is no way to predict the outcome of every situation. We frequently become nervous when we don't know what will happen or what something will entail. One way to calm your nerves and become more confident is to learn about the situation. Take some time to do some research, ask a friend or colleague, or do some online searching. Most people are more than willing to share their experiences and offer advice, if only they are asked. You would be surprised at the amount of people who have already been in your situation, or who can point you in the right direction of someone who can help. If you are going to a job interview, research the company before you go. Go online to do a Google search on interview tips. Ask a trusted friend or colleague for tips on how they present themselves in an interview, or for key points on how to dress if you are unsure. Just knowing that someone else is in your corner and that you are not alone can make all the difference in transferring your nervous energy into confidence.

Keep a Journal

Keeping a journal is a tried and true method that helps reduce stress and anxiety and can help focus that nervous energy on a positive mission. When you keep a journal, you are doing something creative, which benefits the brain. Writing about events in your life, even if you only write for a few minutes a day, provides a release for your emotions. It has been proven that putting pen to paper and allowing your brain to flow naturally is good for improving creativity and reducing stress. When you write, your brain is connected to your hand, and your hand flows freely, letting your mind go. Keeping a journal and writing things down can help you process your thoughts. Writing things down is a good way to keep track of daily events and allows you to go back and reflect on your experiences and

Chapter 3: Learn Psychological Factors That Help You View Setbacks as Opportunities

thoughts. You might be amazed at the progress you see in just a short amount of time, and once this progress is recorded on paper, you can see the changes and improvements right in front of your eyes. Journaling also allows you to brainstorm, coming up with new ideas and outlooks on things. You might think your life is not worth writing about, but once you begin to write, letting the creative juices flow, new ideas will emerge, and you will develop a new outlook on things. In addition to tracking your daily events, you can also use your journal to write about how you reacted to these events. By writing about your emotions, you are getting them out of your head and not allowing them to stay pent up inside. You can look back at the progress you have made, both emotionally and in the way you overcome obstacles. You can celebrate your successes and track your progress. Getting your feelings down on paper allows you to process that nervous energy and reflect on what is causing it. By reflecting on your feelings and understanding what your brain is thinking, you are improving your emotional intelligence, and using that energy for good.

Mental Toughness

Spend Time with Friends or Loved Ones

Humans are pack animals by nature, and human interaction is key to a happy, fulfilling life. It is nice to feel loved, and spending time with old friends, sharing inside jokes and telling stories is a major confidence booster. Our friends and families understand us and have been with us through thick and thin. When spending time with close friends and family, we often feel that we don't have to put on a façade; we can simply be ourselves. Spending time with those who appreciate us automatically gives us a great feeling and a boost of confidence. We all have that one friend or family member who can make any experience a good time. Time spent with this person is full of non-stop laughter, and you often find you are in a much better mood after you leave their company. As it turns out, laughter has several health benefits, including stress-relief. Laughing, especially that deep belly-laugh has been proven to improve circulation, reduce stress, and give you an overall relaxed feeling. Laughter also releases endorphins and serotonin, which are chemicals in the brain associated with happiness and satisfaction. Those people who laugh regularly also have

Chapter 3: Learn Psychological Factors That Help You View Setbacks as Opportunities

healthier immune systems and make better life choices. Happy, laughing people tend to attract other healthy, laughing people. Laughter brings people closer together, and we tend to see our friends and family more frequently when we feel close to them. When you surround yourself with like people, you feel valued and appreciated, and your confidence is boosted.

Learn a New Task or Skill

If you are feeling nervous, another good way to harness that energy and build your self-confidence is by learning a new task or skill. Occupying your mind and forcing yourself to focus on something other than what is bothering you is a great way to reduce some of that nervous energy and improve your self-confidence. If there is a hobby you have always been interested in but never learned how to do, now is the time to focus your energy in that direction. Keeping your mind occupied and removing yourself from the situation of whatever is making you nervous is a great way to get over these feelings. By removing yourself from the situation, you will be able to return later with a fresh perspective, and learning something new is a great way to focus your energy. By practicing a new craft, watching a YouTube video to learn how to do something, or simply reading up on a new subject, you are occupying your mind and switching gears. Not only will this newfound knowledge be beneficial in your life, but you will feel a sense of accomplishment knowing that you have learned something new. Crossing things off your bucket list is the ultimate confidence-booster. Improving your confidence, becoming knowledgeable about a new hobby or skill, and then being able to share your newfound knowledge with others is a great way to harness and refocus your energy, giving you an ultimate rise in confidence and satisfaction.

Eliminate Unwanted Activities or Duties

In this day and age, it becomes extremely easy to overbook our schedules and overcommit to things that we deem priorities. Before you know it, you have something planned for every evening of the week and you are left with none of the much-needed alone time that is valuable in decompressing and de-stressing. Since you are overbooked this week, you are in and out of your house so quickly that the path from your front

Chapter 3: Learn Psychological Factors That Help You View Setbacks as Opportunities

door to your kitchen counter is littered with the shoes you threw off and the junk mail you didn't open yet. By the end of the week, it becomes easy to feel exhausted, run-down, and over-extended. The clutter only adds to your level of stress and anxiety. If you are feeling overextended, take some time to consider whether or not all of these social obligations are really necessary. Yes, sometimes we all have a busy week, but there are some things we could clear from our calendar and not think twice about. Take a few minutes to analyze your social calendar and determine whether or not you are actually looking forward to each and every one of these activities. If there is an event that you are not excited about, or even worse, an event you are dreading, make the decision to rescind your RSVP.

Being assertive and setting boundaries are an integral part of emotional intelligence, and your confidence will skyrocket once you can achieve these goals and free up your schedule. Not only will your confidence surge from your ability to be assertive and set boundaries, but you will have more free time to focus on other confidence-boosting activities, such as learning a new skill, journaling, or spending time with friends and loved ones.

Do Something Nice for Someone Else

Another way to eliminate nervous energy and boost your confidence is by doing something nice for someone else. Completing a task for someone else, even if it's something small, can boost your endorphins and leave you, and the other person, elated. Performing a nice task allows you to focus your energy on something positive and keep your mind off your worries as well. When you help someone else out, whether it's by sharing your knowledge to help them solve a problem, or by completing an actual task, you are taking your mind off of your worries and focusing your energy elsewhere. Once you are finished with the task, you might have a new perspective on your original problem, or you might simply have exerted all of your energy, spending that nervous energy wisely. An additional bonus of doing something nice for someone else is that feeling of appreciation you will get from that person. When they bestow their thanks upon you, you feel appreciated and loved, and that boosts your self-confidence as well.

Chapter 3: Learn Psychological Factors That Help You View Setbacks as Opportunities

Exercise

Get rid of that nervous energy with a trip to the gym. It's a well-known fact that exercise is beneficial in many areas of your life, so next time you feel like you could run around the block with all that pen up nervous energy, it might behoove you to lace up those running shoes and do exactly that. In addition to eliminating some of that nervous energy, exercise is also a key confidence booster, but most likely in more ways than you might think. Exercise is a key component in the reduction of stress. Not only does it work off some of that energy, but it also reduces stress by boosting endorphins. Just a few short workout sessions a week can be as beneficial as taking an anti-depressant. When you are under less stress, your confidence is boosted, and you have an overall more positive outlook on life. Increased confidence comes from not only from the chemicals in your brain but also from your physical appearance as well. When you exercise your clothes fit better, and you look better, which ultimately boosts your confidence. Exercise increases blood flow, which in turn gives you a healthy glow. Exercise has also been proven to boost brain power, which can benefit and enhance self-confidence.

De-clutter

One solution that is often overlooked in the many methods of reducing nervous energy is the simple act of de-cluttering. Getting rid of junk mail, keeping everything in its place, and keeping an overall tidy home is a relatively simple way to de-stress and keep nervous energy at bay. When you are surrounded by or living in an untidy atmosphere, it can be nerve-wracking trying to find your keys each morning before work or your favorite pair of shoes to complete your outfit. If everything has its place and you know where to find things, you can eliminate the waste of time and frantic energy you spend trying to find things that you need. The more time you spend running around searching for things frantically, the more your anxiety levels rise. When you are surrounded by clutter, you feel nervous and unorganized, which can, in turn, lower your confidence. If you put yourself in a calm state, you will not force yourself to feel frenzied and out of character. Keeping a sense of

Chapter 3: Learn Psychological Factors That Help You View Setbacks as Opportunities

calm and order in your life is paramount to boosting confidence and emotional intelligence.

Take Your Pet for a Walk

By getting outside and getting a breath of fresh air, a change of scenery, and a change in your thought process, you can reduce nervous energy and refocus your thoughts. Even a quick walk around the block with Fido can be monumental in eliminating nervous energy. Not only are you getting exercise, exerting your nervous energy for good, and increasing your blood flow, but you are taking a break from the task or thing that is causing the stress, allowing yourself to come back after your walk with a fresh outlook. You will enjoy the change of scenery, and your dog will appreciate getting out as well. Taking care of an animal who loves and depends on you is rewarding, and knowing that you are needed can boost your self-confidence as well.

Act Confident

When all else fails, act like you are confident and your brain will eventually believe itself. Acting confident is not the same as acting conceited. A mentally intelligent person knows the difference between confidence and cockiness, and he or she will display their behavior to reflect this knowledge. Keep your values and beliefs intact and remain willing to listen to other people and their suggestions. Changing your body language can have a monumental effect on your self-confidence and the way that others perceive you. By standing tall, walking with a purpose, and not crossing your arms when sitting or standing, you are tricking your brain into thinking that you are confident. Look at yourself in the mirror and recite affirmative statements in your head. By displaying these actions and hearing affirmative words, your brain will start to believe what it sees and hears, and you will feel and act with a higher level of self-confidence.

Enhance Visualization Techniques and Learn to Create Success Imagery That Will Generate Powerful Results

Picturing success is just the first step to achieving success. People who are successful in life do not let themselves picture anything but success. Creating success imagery is vital to improving self-confidence and emotional intelligence. You may have heard stories of little

Chapter 3: Learn Psychological Factors That Help You View Setbacks as Opportunities

elderly ladies lifting cars off their grandchildren after a car accident. Although this superhuman feat of strength is attributed to the adrenaline rush in the heat of the moment, at no point in time did the person question or doubt that she could lift the car to save a life. She knew what had to be done at the moment and then reacted quickly without a second thought. Your success imagery and visualization techniques should be exactly that-no room for second guesses or doubts. You know what you want your end goal to look like, and that's the image that should remain in your head as a constant.

Before you can begin your road to success, you must picture what you want success to look like. Everyone wants to be successful, but success looks different to some people. Do you imagine that to be successful you must own a mansion, drive an expensive car, and make a six-figure salary? Or do you define success as owning your own home and working in a career you enjoy? The meaning and picture of success can be different for everyone, and that's okay. But before you can make a vague goal about wanting to be successful in life, you should first determine what you want success to look like.

Mental Toughness

The image you picture in your head might be completely different from where you are in life now, and this too is okay. You must be willing to work hard and put in the necessary steps to create your own success. This is where your mental toughness and emotional intelligence will come into play. You should picture yourself accomplishing your goal, no matter what you encounter and what obstacles you will face. Picturing success boosts confidence, and confidence is what will lead you to be successful.

Creating success imagery takes training practice. You have to train your brain to think in terms of success, especially if you are making some changes in your life from where you currently are now. Odds are if you are dreaming of success, you are not happy with where you are now in life, and that is okay too. The first step in realizing you want to achieve more success is to realize just that-that you want to achieve more success. If you already know that you want to make a change in one or more areas of your life, then you have already taken the first step.

The mind is a powerful tool, and we can use our brain and the images we produce to either help

Chapter 3: Learn Psychological Factors That Help You View Setbacks as Opportunities

or hinder us. The images we see of ourselves often determine the reality of our situation. Many females have teetered around in high heels, paranoid about tripping and falling in front of a crowd of people. They become so obsessed with the vision of themselves tripping over their heels and falling in front of a crowd of people, and that image in their brain ultimately becomes a self-fulfilling prophecy. On the opposite end of the spectrum, athletes who use visualization techniques to create success imagery often picture themselves winning a game or competition and will ultimately win said game or competition because it becomes so ingrained in their brain that they can't imagine a scenario in which winning does not occur.

When you picture completing a task or achieving a goal in your head, your brain automatically releases the same responses it would as if you had already completed the task at hand. After you begin this practice of positive mental imagery, visualization techniques, and success imagery, you will begin to believe it yourself, and your body will respond automatically as if there is no other option for an outcome.

Picturing yourself succeeding is monumental to improving and maintaining self-esteem. Positive mental images can also reduce stress because you are picturing your success instead of worrying about failure and all the aftermath that comes with it. Use affirmative language when speaking not only to yourself but to your friends and family as well. If you have shared your goals with others, use language when speaking about your goal that does not allow for failure. Use phrases such as, "When I..." "I will..." "I can't wait to..." etc.

You have already begun part of the process- realizing that you want to change and making choices in your life to determine how you will actually make these changes. Success imagery is a powerful tool and can be used in a multitude of ways. Before you begin to make the change toward success, you should first choose a specific end goal. What do you want to accomplish? Do you want to publish a book? Earn a degree? Complete your Master's program?

Once you have your end goal in sight, break that goal into smaller, more attainable goals. If you want to write a book, determine how many

Chapter 3: Learn Psychological Factors That Help You View Setbacks as Opportunities

paragraphs, pages, or chapters you can accomplish at any given time. Make your goal realistic so that you do not set yourself up for failure. If you know your schedule will realistically only allow you to finish a chapter a week, make that your goal. Picture in your head where you will do your writing, what time of day you will write, and the literal process of how you will accomplish this. Will you type everything out on in Microsoft Word, saving along the way, or will you write in a notebook first so that you have the creative freedom to just let your brain flow? Although these may sound like minor details, these are the types of things you must break down to set your realistic goal. The more details you can imagine, the better the process will work for you.

After you have broken down your end goal into smaller, more manageable chunks, write these smaller goals out. Make a list of everything you need to accomplish for each goal, including the time it will take to accomplish the smaller goals.

Include all five senses in your success imagery. What will it feel like to have finally accomplished your goal? Of course, you will feel like a weight has been lifted off your shoulders, but what other emotions will you feel? Happiness, pride, a sense of accomplishment, and a boost in self-confidence are imminent. When you do accomplish this goal, what sounds will you hear, what smells will you smell, what will you taste, and what will you see? If your book is published, you might smell the fresh pages of a new novel, hear the congratulatory message from your husband on the phone, taste the celebratory champagne you share with your best friend, see your book on the shelves in the bookstore, and feel the weight of the book in your hand or the pen you use to autograph a copy of your book. Picturing the entire scenario from beginning to end and every little detail will improve your confidence and will give you a positive push in the right direction.

You have already imagined how you will feel once you accomplish your own goal, but now imagine how your goal would feel through the eyes of a bystander or loved one. What would it be like for a spectator to be in the audience as you give your successful speech or book talk? What questions might they ask you and how will you respond? What would an aerial view of your

Chapter 3: Learn Psychological Factors That Help You View Setbacks as Opportunities

success look like, or what would your success look like through the eyes of someone who was interviewing you and telling your story? Picturing your success, using visualization techniques and success imagery from every angle will give you a firm grasp on your goal and will further cement the success in your brain. With all the positive images from every angle, there is no way you can fail.

Celebrate your milestones along the way. You have an end goal in sight, but each of the smaller goals you have set is a goal that you are accomplishing as well, so it's important to give yourself credit for this as well. Celebrating your smaller achievements along the way will also boost your self-confidence, which will be even more motivation to keep moving towards the end goal.

Have a backup plan for any hurdles you might encounter. Successful, confident people know that all success does not always come without some disappointment and failure along the way. The mentally tough person views obstacles as a learning process and sees failures as an opportunity to revamp and revise their existing plan. He or she knows there will be unexpected situations that crop up along the way, and they usually have a plan to resolve these issues. Keeping the end goal and your successful images in mind, think about what hurdles you might overcome and how you can overcome these hurdles. If your goal is to write a novel and you want to write a chapter a week, think about how you can manage your time. Can you wake up thirty minutes earlier each day while your household is still quiet so that you can have some time for yourself to write? Can you leave your phone out of reach while you write so that you are not tempted to check Facebook or Instagram? Try to anticipate what roadblocks you could encounter and be proactive about fixing these issues before they become a problem.

Odds are, even if you have your end goal in mind, you have your larger goal broken down into smaller goals, and you even have a backup plan for your backup plan, you will still need to fix some problems, especially if you have a lengthy or detailed goal in mind. There is nothing wrong with revising your goal and revamping your method, or even starting

Chapter 3: Learn Psychological Factors That Help You View Setbacks as Opportunities

completely over from scratch, as long as you don't beat yourself up over the process. Everyone makes mistakes, and these mistakes can be a jumping off point that will lead you in a whole different direction. Mentally tough people know that they can change their plan and still be successful in the end. Mentally tough people keep their success image in sight and their end goal in mind.

Understand What to Practice and Which Success Conditioning Exercises Vastly Improve Performance

Just like your body needs to work out physically to stay in top shape, your brain needs a workout also. By practicing mental conditioning exercises, your brain will develop self-affirming thoughts and a higher-level of self-confidence almost automatically. Soon, positive thoughts and mental images will become a habit, and your brain will automatically be programmed for success.

As you previously learned, our thoughts can affect our lives in many ways. What we think we eventually do or become, and positive thoughts will only allow for positive experiences and outcomes. Our thoughts affect our emotions, which affect our actions, which affect our goals. Harboring negative thoughts leads to negative emotions, which lead to negative actions, or sometimes inaction. On the opposite end of the spectrum, positive thoughts lead to positive emotions, which lead to positive actions, which leads us to achieve our goals and increase our self-confidence.

Practicing good mental conditioning not only keeps us mentally and physically healthy, but also improves our self-confidence, increases our ability to concentrate, and reduces stress. Mental conditioning takes practice, but if you believe it, you can achieve it. By now you have learned that the mind is a powerful tool that you have with you at all times. When you are in peak mental condition, your self-confidence improves because you know you can achieve your goals. You can concentrate because you have a goal in mind and you know what it takes to achieve that goal. Your stress levels are down because you have an end goal in mind and have taken the steps to perform the end goal. You know what needs to be done and you have pictured yourself

Chapter 3: Learn Psychological Factors That Help You View Setbacks as Opportunities

achieving said goal. Your feelings of stress and anxiety have all but disappeared because you are no longer frantic about achieving success and living your dreams. You know exactly what you need to accomplish to get there. This might sound like a foreign language to you, or at the very least, a little far-fetched. If you have just recently decided your brain and mental state could use a workout, then the following tips will be very beneficial to you. If you have been coaching yourself along the way, keep reading, as a refresher course is always a good reminder of how you can improve your thoughts and increase your mental strength so that you can achieve even more than you thought possible.

Take away surrounding factors so that you are forced into a new experience. This might sound unpleasant to you at first, but by removing external factors and pushing yourself to try something new, you have already taken a step forward out of your comfort zone. You will surprise yourself with what you can accomplish. For example, let's say you just started going to the gym. You might have been an athlete back in high school, but the obligations of a house, career, and family have gotten in the way of your fitness routine, and now you must backtrack to regain progress. Congratulations! The first step is knowing that you need to make a change. You have been working out at the gym in small increments of time, running on the treadmill and using the elliptical machine. Your friend is running a 5K and suggests that you should run with her next month. You are unsure how you feel about running in front of people and do not feel like you can compete, but against your better judgment, you sign up. You have already taken that first step out of your comfort zone. The first step is often the hardest, so there is nowhere to go but up from here. You begin to train so that you can run the entire three-point-one miles without stopping. You imagine yourself crossing the finish line and receiving the medal passed out by the race organization. Race day arrives, and you pace yourself appropriately and take it one mile at a time. You do successfully cross the finish line with a much faster time than you thought possible. Congratulations, again! You have forced yourself out of your comfort zone, tried a new experience, and felt a sense of accomplishment when you crossed the finish line. By breaking the race into manageable segments and picturing yourself succeeding, you

Chapter 3: Learn Psychological Factors That Help You View Setbacks as Opportunities

did exactly that. You will surprise yourself with what you can accomplish when you put your mind to it and picture success.

Stick to a routine. Mental toughness and routine go hand in hand. Sticking to a routine is an important part of maintaining mental toughness. By sticking to a routine, you can plan out your day and allow for time if something does not go as planned. Creating your own routine allows you take control of your day and your schedule so that you can make the necessary changes. Keeping your routine and then crossing things off your list as you go through your day gives you a feeling of accomplishment and also boosts your self-confidence. Your feeling of success and accomplishment is directly related to your mental strength.

Don't let things bother you that you have no control over. We all have busy lives, and sometimes you just have to roll with the punches. We don't know what is going on in anyone else's head at any given point in time. That person who cut you off in traffic? They could very well have been late to pick up a sick kid from school. The person glaring at you at the grocery store? They might have been annoyed that the store was out of their favorite brand of salad dressing and just happened to be glaring in your direction as you walked by. The point is, we can only control our own actions and emotions, and if we let the actions and emotions of other people dictate our lives, we would never accomplish anything. Mentally strong people know that they control their own destiny and that it's up to themselves to take action and control of the situation. Situations in our workplace, the weather, and how others treat us are results of external factors, but mentally strong people know it's how we react to those situations that help improve our mental strength.

Get Rid of Limiting Beliefs and the Negative Critic in Your Head Once and For All

It is often said that we are our own worst critics. While we are sure that people are looking at us and criticizing or making fun, the reality of it is that no one is probably paying that much attention to what you see as imperfections. A mentally strong person will get rid of their self-

Chapter 3: Learn Psychological Factors That Help You View Setbacks as Opportunities

limiting beliefs and not dwell on negative things. Eliminate those negative thoughts by replacing the thoughts with positive images and self-affirming language. Negative thoughts come from the feeling that you are losing control of a situation and will flounder in the aftermath. Negative thoughts also come from a feeling of uncertainty and the fear of the unknown. When something unexpected happens, such as a job loss, we do not know what will happen next. The unknown is scary, and the feeling of uncertainty is what causes the anxious feeling. A mentally strong person will take action to view yet another change as a challenge, and will take steps to derail their negative train of thought.

Alter your body language. Altering body language is a quick fix to eliminate that pesky internal critic. Stand up straight, uncross your arms, and hold your head tall. A confident posture will trick your mind and body into believing that you are confident.

Make a list of things to be thankful for. While it may be easy to get caught up in negative images, there is plenty around you to be thankful for. Make a list of things that you have accomplished recently or a list of people and things in your life for which you are grateful. Writing things down gives your brain a chance to brainstorm and think creatively, which will improve your self-image and bring about positive thoughts.

Do something creative. Start a craft project or work in your garden. Using your creativity boosts self-confidence and improves your mood. Once your creative juices are flowing, and you are completing an activity that you enjoy, your brain will recognize this and produce the appropriate chemicals to make you feel happy. When you are doing something creative, your self-confidence increases and your happiness returns. Happiness attracts happiness, and your negative thoughts and self-doubt will soon disappear.

A final way to get rid of these negative thoughts is to replace these thoughts with positive, self-affirming thoughts. Allow yourself to feel the negative thought and recognize why you feel that way or are feeling this sense of fear, and then replace the thought with a positive one. Picture yourself grabbing the thought and releasing it, then replace the thought with a positive thought that gives you a more desirable outcome. If you

Chapter 3: Learn Psychological Factors That Help You View Setbacks as Opportunities

are afraid, you will trip in front of a crowd of people, release that thought from your head and picture yourself walking calmly in front of the crowd and straight to your destination.

Eliminating negative thoughts and training your brain to think positively is something that comes over time. You must first recognize when you are thinking negative thoughts and determine what is causing the thoughts to enter your head. By practicing these techniques, they will soon become a habit. Mentally strong people know that it is up to them to embrace these challenges and change their lives for the better.

Chapter 4:
Improve Focus and Concentration for Positive Results with Battle Training Mental Techniques

It is a well-known fact that members of any branch of the military today are some of the most battle-hardened, top-conditioned people in the country. Military personnel go through a grueling training program that produces some of the most mentally and physically tough people in our country. To complete these programs, the prospective soldier must first be emotionally intelligent and have strong mental health. He or she will use these qualities to complete their training and become even stronger, both physically and mentally, than they were before. Just as soldiers are trained in this manner, top professional athletes are trained in this manner as well. A professional athlete lives, breathes, dreams his or her sport, and just endures grueling days of physical challenges to revel in the spotlight of a two-hour game.

Gain Insight into the Coaching Psychology Behind Redirecting Anger Energy

Anger shows itself on many different levels. Some people are more apt to show anger than others. Although anger can be viewed as a negative emotion with a negative connotation, in truth, anger can be used for good when it is directed the right way. Everyone feels anger, but it is what we do with that anger that can determine the outcome.

When anger is used in a negative manner, it can halt success because too much time is wasted on feeling the emotion. People who cannot control their anger often pause what they are doing, feel the rage, and then are forced to redirect their attention back to the task at hand. When anger is used positively, the surge of energy and adrenaline that is felt in the heat of the moment can be used for good.

A bad call by a ref, an un-sportsmanlike play from an opposing teammate, or even personal error can cause many athletes to feel extreme

Chapter 4: Improve Focus and Concentration for Positive Results with Battle Training Mental Techniques

anger, especially if surrounding circumstances dictate a stressful situation. A big game or tournament or a tough competitor can be just the thing that causes everyone's adrenaline to run high from the beginning. When extenuating circumstances are added to the mix, the first emotion many athletes feel, especially if they are competitive by nature, is anger. When playing sports, coaches often teach athletes to use their anger for good, using the energy as an extra boost to run the extra ten yards, pick up the pace down the court, or spike the volleyball that much harder.

Create an image in your head that will get you through anything. This image is often referred to as the "trigger." The trigger can be anything from your child, to your pet, to your best friend. This trigger is something that you live for and would do anything for. You can redirect your anger by thinking of this trigger to propel you through a difficult situation. Many military personnel envisions this image in their mind to get through a difficult situation or training. The thought of the person or animal at the end of the obstacle often propels the person through and gives them the extra surge of energy needed to complete the difficult task or the strength to go on in difficult times. Coaches instill this same idea by advising their athletes to pick a "trigger" as well. Not only does this technique get athletes through a grueling workout, but it allows the athletes to envision success. Coaches instruct their athletes to picture this trigger in the stands or watching the difficult workout take place. This, in turn, motivates most people to improve their performance, based on the sheer fact that their brain believes this. The athlete will perform better "knowing" that someone whom they are trying to impress is watching them.

Become aware of the situation. Military commanders and coaches alike instill this into their subjects. A tried and true battle technique is to become aware of your surroundings at all times, even if this just means glancing around and observing people in the surrounding area. By becoming aware of the surrounding situation, you can be ready for anything that might happen. All branches of the military instill this in their soldiers because it is important to be alert at all times if a dangerous situation would occur. Coaches instill this in their players as a part of the game. If athletes are aware of other players

Chapter 4: Improve Focus and Concentration for Positive Results with Battle Training Mental Techniques

around them, they can anticipate not only the opponent's next move but their own next move as well. An emotionally intelligent person can observe and identify a situation, determine what they are feeling and why they are feeling these emotions, due to the situation, and then process their emotions and react accordingly. Becoming aware of your surrounding situations is something that comes with a practiced sense of self-awareness. You can practice this technique in any public place, regardless of whether or not you are in a situation that will make you angry. Next time you are sitting in a restaurant, take some time to observe others around you. Do those people sitting near you seem nervous, jittery, or full of energy? Are they tired and sluggish? Are you sitting in close proximity to someone, and if so, does that make you nervous? As you observe and analyze people around you, take note of your own reactions to your situation. Note your feelings and try to determine why you might be feeling what you are feeling. The more in tune you become with yourself, the easier it is to determine why you feel what you are feeling, and how you can use those emotions and reactions to your benefit. The mentally strong person can recognize his or her emotions and can also determine what is making them feel that way.

Use Anger Energy to Strengthen and Resolve Control

Anger is one of the most intense emotions that humans experience, and this can be both good and bad. That extra surge of energy you feel when you are angry can be used to accomplish new things or push yourself farther, as long as you use the feeling in the right way. Of course, too much anger is not a good thing. You know yourself better than anyone, and you can use your self-awareness to determine whether or not your anger is at a normal level for yourself. If you are someone who has an extreme temper and you know you get angry easily, check yourself from time to time to see if this is a normal feeling for you. If the feeling is not normal, check your circumstances and determine what changes can be made before your anger gets out of hand.

Don't become calm. Although this advice may sound counterintuitive, if you truly want to use your anger to produce a positive outcome, trying to calm yourself down completely will not

Chapter 4: Improve Focus and Concentration for Positive Results with Battle Training Mental Techniques

produce the desired effect. The rage you feel is what will cause you to make a change in your life or complete an action. For example, as an athlete, if you had possession of the ball and had been tackled the last three times you ran down the field, you can use this anger to fuel your energy to run faster. A mentally strong person will not get discouraged by this setback of being tackled; rather, he will use this chance to improve his playing skills and will be motivated to run faster. He will picture himself in the end zone, dancing his victory dance after he scores a touchdown. He will imagine how it would feel to hear the crowd cheering, he will imagine how the turf smells, and he will imagine the scoreboard changing, his team's score increasing after he has made the touchdown. He might even go so far as to imagine how the ice-cold water will taste after he runs fast enough to score the touchdown. The moral of the story is, by trying to calm your emotions and remove some of the anger, you are losing some of the ammunition that will ultimately fuel your fire to accomplish your goal.

Use the anger to make a plan. Human beings are emotional creatures, and the anger you feel can be your drive and determination to make a plan.

Mental Toughness

If you are someone who gets annoyed easily, but never does anything to correct the situation, you can use your anger to make a plan. Do not try to calm yourself down, because once you are calm, you will most likely decide that the thing that once made you so angry is no longer a big deal. While your emotions are still running high and you still feel angry, make a plan that will get you out of the situation. If you are at work and your boss has incorrectly blamed you for a mistake, it is wise not to yell or direct the anger towards your boss. Rather, make a plan and use your anger to fuel your actions. Rewrite your cover letter, stating exactly what your qualifications are. Give up your hour of television time each night to begin searching for a new job. The bottom line is, if you try to calm yourself in every situation, you will not be able to reign in your anger to use it productively. Allow yourself to feel the anger, and remember the feelings you felt when the experience happened. Make the determination that you will not allow yourself to be put into this situation again, and resolve to change it. A mentally strong person knows some things in life cannot be controlled, but he or she can determine how they respond to the situation. Recognizing that the emotion they are feeling is

Chapter 4: Improve Focus and Concentration for Positive Results with Battle Training Mental Techniques

anger, identifying the source of the anger, and then making the determination to resolve the solution are all signs of behavior that an emotionally intelligent human being would display.

Decide if it's worth showing your anger. Some things in life are just not worth getting upset about. While it's great to use your anger to make necessary changes in your life, sometimes it is just as important to step back and decide whether or not it is worth getting upset about the situation at hand. An emotionally intelligent person can look at the situation and determine why they are feeling the way they are, and then decide if their emotions are warranted. A good way to put this practice into perspective is to ask yourself how you would feel if someone close to you was telling you the same story. If a close friend or family member had the same scenario happen to them, and they recounted the story to you, how would you feel? Would you be enraged on their behalf, or would you think they were overreacting? This can sometimes be an effective tool in determining whether it is a good idea to use your anger to make a change, or if you should just let the situation drop. An emotionally intelligent person can make the determination between rational and irrational behavior.

Use Proven Sports Technology Techniques to Leave Your Ego Outside

When most people hear the word ego, there is a negative connotation that comes to mind. You might think of a famous musician or athlete who is portrayed in the media as very full of themselves. You might also hear the word ego and think of someone who has an inflated ego, or a big ego. Truthfully, everyone has an ego, but it's when the ego becomes too inflated that problems arise. The ego is your own sense of self-esteem and importance. Some people tend to have high egos and extremely high levels of self-esteem, while still, other people tend to have lower egos and low levels of self-esteem. While it is good to have a sense of self-worth, an overly inflated ego can be annoying to others around you, causing you to lose friends and make family members dread being around you. No one wants to hear about how great you are or how wonderful your athletic ability is every time they see you, but at the same time, an emotionally intelligent and mentally strong person has a

Chapter 4: Improve Focus and Concentration for Positive Results with Battle Training Mental Techniques

great sense of self and a high level of self-esteem. How can we determine the difference, and when our ego gets in the way, how can we leave our ego outside and enter the ring of life in a more humble state?

One way to determine whether someone has an over-active ego is to decide whether or not that person can back up what they are saying with their actions. If a star athlete brags about their skills, yet doesn't deliver peak performance when he is on the basketball court, then his over-inflated ego is getting in the way of this performance and is also hurting his teammates. If the star athlete not only brags about his skills, but then does not deliver on the basketball court, is rude to his teammates and opponents, and disrespectful to his coaches and superiors, then his ego has become over-inflated. As a general rule of thumb, if someone can practice good sportsmanship, they have a high level of confidence and a healthy ego. And in real life, typically someone who is friendly, can get along with others, and can place themselves in others' shoes is someone who has a high confidence level and a healthy ego. Emotionally intelligent and mentally strong people can maintain their self-confidence, yet still participate in competitive activities. They can recognize their emotions and realize when they are feeling a negative emotion, and what might be causing them to feel this way.

While high levels of self-confidence are good, an over-inflated ego is not. There are some proven ways to drop the ego and return to your more humble bearings, and like most strategies used to improve your mental state, these too require practice and patience.

Practice forgiveness. Recognize that not everyone is out to get you. Everyone that you encounter on a daily basis is human, just like you. Circumstances will occur throughout your day that might offend you, but it is how you react to these circumstances that dictate the level of your mental state. Whether someone has intended to offend you or not, practice forgiveness. Forgiving someone for a wrongdoing, whether real or imagined, has a calming effect. It is natural to be upset if someone slams the door in your face or pulls out in front of you at the intersection, but not recognizing that this could be an honest mistake

Chapter 4: Improve Focus and Concentration for Positive Results with Battle Training Mental Techniques

is detrimental to your physical and mental health. If you feel the need to chase the co-worker down the hall at work to in turn slam the door in his face, or chase the offending driver down the street to honk and wave at them, it is time to check your ego. Letting these small things drop and moving on with your day are proveen ways to set your ego aside. You do not always have to be right, and you do not always have to come out on top of every situation.

Additionally, your ego can benefit from forgiving bigger transgressions as well. If a friend or family member unintentionally offended you and then apologizes, you can practice keeping your ego in check by choosing to forgive them. Everyone makes mistakes, and the emotionally healthy and mentally strong person can recognize this and move on with their lives. At the same time, the emotionally healthy person is also able to set boundaries and stand up for themselves, so if this person keeps offending you, you owe it to yourself to enforce the consequences and move on with your life. Forgive the person and realize that you deserve to be treated with respect. It is when you throw a temper tantrum and try to get even with the

Mental Toughness

offending person that the negative side of your ego comes out, causing others to feel like you have an over-inflated sense of self.

One way to keep your ego at a healthy level is to realize you can't control every situation. Every situation in life will not go as planned. The emotionally intelligent person realizes this and makes amends to their plan when they need to, viewing obstacles as new challenges and not complete disasters. People who only want to do things their way, remaining rigid and unchanging, are not allowing themselves to grow as a person. Someone with an over-inflated ego only wants things to be done their way, regardless of how many other people are involved in the decision-making process. By stepping back, letting some things happen naturally, and embracing the challenges that life throws at you, your ego will stay outside, allowing you to enter and experience all life has to offer.

Conclusion

Improving Mental Toughness Will Benefit Every Area of Your Life

Mental toughness is a key component to living a successful, healthy life. It is normal for everyone to experience setbacks in life, and sometimes we go through a period of time in our lives that is more challenging than other times. It is what we do with these challenges that can vastly impact our lives. By achieving and maintaining a high level of emotional intelligence, we can recognize and alter our reactions to fit the situation, as well as to benefit ourselves in the long run. By practicing the acts of believing and relying on our intuition, setting boundaries, adhering to a schedule, and eliminating the fear of rejection, we can effectively reduce anxiety and in turn, boost self-esteem.

When things do not go our way, we can choose to use these unfavorable opportunities as a chance to grow and change, or we can choose to let ourselves be struck down by these situations, remaining in a rut and feeling stuck. When we have too many negative circumstances in our lives, it is only natural for us to feel the intense emotion of anger, but it is what we do with that anger that can turn our lives around for the better. Learning to harness our anger and use this extra energy can be a monumental, life-altering strategy. The practice of training your brain and using proven psychological techniques has been shown to be beneficial to athletes and military personnel, and you too can learn to employ these methods to improve the quality of your life, your self-esteem, and your overall mental health.

Improving your mental toughness will get you through a tough work day, will help you determine the appropriate response to adverse events, and will improve your overall self-confidence. Maintaining a high level of self-confidence is paramount to living a healthy, happy life. Improving your mental strength not only improves your life but the lives of others around you. Your friends and family will notice the change in your overall demeanor and your happiness, as will you. Happy people tend to

Conclusion

attract happy people, and people who display a healthy ego, a high level of self-confidence, and terrific mental toughness are often more sought-after in the workplace. These same people also tend to make and keep true friendships and relationships, as they can set boundaries and enjoy a balance of personal time and time spent with others.

Mental toughness is not something that can be learned overnight; it takes practice and determination to change your mindset and adjust your way of thinking. The good news is, if you have found the need for improvement in your mental health, you have already taken a step in the right direction.

www.ingramcontent.com/pod-product-compliance
Lightning Source LLC
Chambersburg PA
CBHW020913080526
44589CB00011B/581